SUSCEPTIBLE TO LIGHT

Poetry

by

Chelan Harkin

Cover design by Jordan Blumer blumerjordan@gmail.com

DEDICATION

I dedicate this book to Sheri, one of my heart's favorite places to rest and restore its inherent merriment. And to Asa, my sweetheart muse in the Great Beyond.

CONTENTS

ACKNOWLEDGMENTS

Where to begin? I'll start with my teachers and those who introduced me to poetry and fanned its flame within me: my mom, Rene Weiler, who offered me $20 to memorize The Cloud by Percy Bysshe Shelley at age five and to my Grandpa James for that poem being his favorite. To my dad, Bill Weiler, for being the most creatively uninhibited person I know. To all my ancestors with sensitive spirits for whom beauty found its way in and nourished the ancestral pot to pass down to me the great inheritance of a soul that is susceptible to light. To Shirlee Jellum, my high school creative writing teacher, to Paul Woolery, my first therapist, who read me my first Hafiz poem in a session that began to break me open, to my college professor Hirsh Diamant who believed in my poetry and gave it space to share itself more widely. To Fred LaMotte, one of my great mentors and inspirations.

Then there are those who meaningfully and directly helped this book to be created: Tina Benson, without whom I'd still be waiting for a publisher to land on my head, my husband, Noah Harkin, for his multifaceted loving support, to Rob Clack for helping me find the fabulous title font for each poem in this book, to Justin Larson for helping me activate my passions and prioritize bringing this book to life, to Jordan Blumer for her excellent cover design, to Elizabeth de Souza for her endorsement and all around fabulousness, to David Hunt and JB Eckl, two creative wizards, for loving my poetry and saying so.

And to all my many readers over the years who have let my words enter them and who have expressed their love for my poetry. I cannot thank you enough or express fully what this has meant to me. Lastly, I gotta thank Hafiz, my primary poetic inspiration.

INTRODUCTION

Great poetry can induce any number of emotions in the reader, from pain and anguish, to longing and love. What mystic poetry does, ala Rumi, Rilke, and Hafiz, is induce a state of wonderment, awe, mystery, and innocence...a willingness to relinquish all we have already decided about ourselves and existence, and meet the moment wholly anew, allowing life to reveal itself to us in its full and holy sacredness. Such are the poems in this most delightful collection from poetess Chelan Harkin. Her poems return us to our original innocence...to the wonder of discovery that is our birthright. Harkin invites the reader to, "Break yourself down into the basic components of primitive awe and let the crescendo of each moment carbonate every capillary and say, 'Wow!'" This is a beautiful compilation of WOWS! Let yourself be carried away on this ecstatic current of wonder-drenched poems and you will surely find your heart singing and dancing with each and every beautiful offering.

—Tina M. Benson, M.A,

international bestselling author of *A Woman Unto Herself: A Different Kind of Love Story*

LEAVE YOUR SHOES

Leave your shoes

and your old concepts of God

at the door.

Hang your heavy identities

on the coat rack—

you simply don't need those things in here!

It's much too warm in this house

for all the facade you've been bundling up in.

If you come with pain

let's use it to light a fire

in this old hearth.

Sharing this flame

puts it in its rightful place

where our humanity can gather

around it together

and sing!

Leave your shoes

and your old concepts of God

at the door

and let's see what wonders emerge

when we let our souls and our feet free

to finally begin

to dance!

"WHY ARE YOU SO HAPPY?"

"Why are you so happy?"

someone asked me.

"Why am I so happy?

Darling, why are you so drab!?"

Birds just threw themselves

into the sky

like a handful of winged seeds

to go pollinate the south with music!

Each evening the sun creates

a symphony of color and your heart matches it!!

I've got two hands that can hold your soft face and magical eyes

with black holes in the middle of them

that spend their whole lives

pulling in all light and beauty!

Because even the winter snag is shimmering with secret promise and I can see a hint of its fruits,

because every bucket of your darkness

is alchemized into wisdom

simply by handing it to the light!

When we were born,

God gave us an automatically refillable bag of jewels called a soul

that we can share with any living thing to make it sparkle

and sing!

Darling, why am I so happy?

Simply because today I am choosing to remember

all of that.

CROWN CHAKRA

You uncorked

my crown chakra

and poured God through me.

Now I'm sodden with music,

dripping poetry.

You've gone away

but I'm still

traipsing golden footprints

over every part

of this once unenchanted world.

You left me with a treasure map.

My soul is now plundering

the abundance of this life—

each atom has become

a jewel.

I WANT MORE OF THAT

I had my first taste of love tonight

for the Essence that made rain-forests

water, trees and time.

I had my first taste of love tonight

for that Essence of unimaginable intelligence

that sang stars and orbits and the immense

tiny perfections

of all the creatures in the sea

into being.

I had my first taste of love tonight

for that Essence that was gracious

and giving and unimaginably tender enough

to have created me,

to have thought me up and said,

"Her. I want to see what her blossom

looks like. I desire her

style of light."

I had my first taste of love tonight

for that genius of love

that makes flowers ache

toward light

and hearts that do the same.

I had my first taste of that sweet, sweet

love tonight for the Essence

that made all the innumerable tidbits

of majesty

sprouting from every wondrous pocket

of this sacred world.

I had my first taste of Divine love tonight

and let's just say,

I want more of that.

HAFIZ WAS GENEROUS

Hafiz was generous.

I asked him for help with my poetry

and he stuffed my heart with a thousand suns

for starters.

He poured a collection of instruments into my soul

and announced, "Play!"

He spit shined my inner eye

that it might see wild magic everywhere

winking back at it.

I asked Hafiz for help with my poetry

and he responded, "It's about time you asked!

I've been waiting with a stampede of muses

to unleash upon you.

I've been waiting with

a cosmos of roses

to hand to you

to bring forth

even the shiest part of your love

and get it dancing!"

I asked Hafiz for help with my poetry.

He said, "All poems already are,

like luminous birds in the spirit realm.

You simply must summon them."

And he started wildly throwing bird food

directly into my soul!

There's a secret trap door in heaven.

When you pull on that string

God topples down upon you.

I asked Hafiz for help with my poetry

and he pushed God out that door

to land right on top

of my heart.

ECSTATIC DRUM

I used to have a hard time

waking in the morning

under the weight of so many

shoulds and responsibilities.

And now, look!

How easy it is for me to rise

now that all there is for me to do

is whirl!

Friend, thank you for turning

this whole dutifully spinning world

into a wild dervish.

Thank you for turning my dutifully

thudding heart

into the ecstatic drum

this whole world

is dancing to.

ARRANGED MARRIAGE

This life is an arranged marriage

between you

and your own soul!

You might resist this for years

rebel against it

and throw a huge fit.

"I wanted him!"

"What about her?!"

But when you finally get in

to that bridal chamber

you'll discover every intimacy

with "the other"

is found here.

WHO SAID I?

Who said I

get to perceive

the spectrum of color

glistening off

of a rainbow trout?

Who said I get to reach

into the body of summer

to claim the sweetness

of a watermelon?

Who said I

get the smooth taste

of sunshine

covering all of my skin

at once?

And who said I

get to be the carrier

of warm rivers

of blood

flowing to and from

the holy ocean

of my heart?

Who said I

get to land

on this soft, fertile orb

floating peaceful circles

around a Dazzling Light?

Who said I

get handed

a handful of years

to make any kind

of beautiful sense of?

Who said I

get the precious work

of un-puzzling closeness

between myself and all of you

and who said I get to ask this

great and mysterious question:

Who said *I*?

Who said *I*?

Who said *I*?

SNUGGLE

Stop trying

to have an extra deep

conversation with the Universe.

Stop trying

to make it all meaningful

and force a connection.

Just admit it, things have been

a little awkward lately.

Let's just get honest:

All you and the Great Mystery

want to do with each other

is curl up close and warm

in fetal position together

and snuggle.

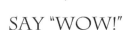

SAY "WOW!"

Each day before our surroundings

become flat with familiarity

and the shapes of our lives click into place,

dimensionless and average as Tetris cubes,

before hunger knocks from our bellies

like a cantankerous old man

and the duties of the day stack up like dishes

and the architecture of our basic needs

commissions all thought

to construct the 4-door sedan of safety,

before gravity clings to our skin

like a cumbersome parasite

and the colored dust of dreams

sweeps itself obscure in the vacuum of reason,

each morning before we wrestle the world

and our hearts into the shape of our brains,

look around and say, "Wow!"

Feed yourself fire.

Scoop up the day entire

like a planet-sized bouquet of marvel

sent by the Universe directly into your arms

and say, "Wow!"

Break yourself down

into the basic components of primitive awe

and let the crescendo of each moment

carbonate every capillary

and say, "Wow!"

Yes, before our poems become calloused

with revision

let them shriek off the page of spontaneity

and before our metaphors get too regular,

let the sun stay

a conflagration of homing pigeons

that fights through fire

each day to find us.

WINO

Leave your heart

in God's cellar,

it will mature there.

This is Grace:

when your heart

makes everything

so sweet with drunkenness

that God,

that Notorious Wino,

visits you often.

LEGLESS PILGRIM

O God, or Unimagined Color, or Colossal Bowl of Lucky

Charms, or Whatever Greatness Happens to be Listening,

I want a rushing river of purity

to carve out my canyons

like the Missoula floods

or a triumphant, God-sized

portion of liquid plumber

to stir up old sediment

without judgment or guilt

and carry it away on its impartial currents.

I want to be clay

in the hands of the seasons,

let them shape me as they please

and I want to not object, nay, to trust

every twig and flower and frostbite

they mold into me.

I want to be emptied, damn-it!

of everything I think I know and don't know

and pulse with that emptiness

like our raw mass of earth before

it was sophisticated into shape and name.

Hold me upside down God,

by my legs or the seat of my pants

and haze me into existence.

Give me a cosmic swirly,

put me in the divine trash can

just let me know I'm here

and that you're involved.

In case you haven't noticed,

I'm not autotrophic

but I've been trying

to be as recklessly self-subsistent as possible

and my harvest has been piss-poor.

I'm ready to come down now

from the high flung, volatile seas

of ego, but the hard edges of facade

have scuffed me up and I'm in no

condition to knock on your door.

But if I have to be a legless pilgrim
I'll still make the trip
stripped to the skivvies
of the lowest denominator
of common truth
though I may be.

But when I arrive,
please, God, forget your manners.
Don't be delicate or proper.
Virtue aside, let's be real—
all I'll want is a big bear hug
and a gluttonous portion
of your heartiest stew.

ENOUGH'S ENOUGH

Let go

of your dysfunctional relationship

with God.

Just say, "enough's enough."

and move out.

Your idea

that God wants you

to feel shame and guilt—

that's the first

warning sign.

Don't assume you're bound

to a necessary

lasting contract

of fear—

what God worth loving

would want that?

Let go of the idea

that this whole, glorious world

isn't spun of golden light

and trust, as you do,

that something much more luminous

is waiting everywhere

to fill you.

I AM LIGHT

What is this acumen

we've developed

to describe our terrors?

Why are our stories of pain

so well carved and whittled?

Why these PhD certificates

of our errors

hanging all over ourselves?

No matter what the degree

of joy, of beauty

why not give ourselves over to that?

No matter how far we are

from where we are aiming to go,

why not look at it differently?

Why not say,

"I am light

building a kingdom of myself."

GO FORTH AND SPILL!

"If you're willing

to do your own clean up work

it doesn't matter what kind of mess you make!"

I said to my three year old.

I think I remember God

whispering the same thing to me

just before incarnation.

"Go forth and spill, darling!

See what is created

from your beautiful, fearless mess!"

THE WORST THING

The worst thing we ever did
was put God in the sky
out of reach,

pulling the divinity
from the leaf,
sifting out the holy from our bones,
insisting God isn't bursting dazzlement through everything
we've made
a hard commitment to see as ordinary,
stripping the sacred from everywhere
to put in a cloud man elsewhere,
prying closeness from your heart.

The worst thing we ever did
was take the dance and the song
out of prayer
made it sit up straight
and cross its legs

removed it of rejoicing

wiped clean its hip sway,

its questions,

its ecstatic yowl,

its tears.

The worst thing we ever did is pretend God isn't the easiest thing

in this universe

available to every soul

in every breath.

I NO LONGER PRAY

I no longer pray—
now I drink dark chocolate
and let the moon sing to me.

I no longer pray—
I let my ancestors dance
through my hips
at the slightest provocation.

I no longer pray—
I go to the river
and howl my ancient pain
into the current.

I no longer pray—
I ache, I desire,
I say "yes" to my longing.

I no longer pray as I was taught

but as the stars crawl

onto my lap like soft animals at nighttime

and God tucks my hair behind my ears

with the gentle fingers of her wind

and a new intimacy is uncovered in everything,

perhaps it's that I'm finally learning

how to pray.

MOTHER

Expand the word, "Mother".

Let it encompass the hills,

the morning,

that which feeds you.

Mother is much too big a word

for one person alone to hold.

Take it off her shoulders.

Hand it to community,

warm baths,

anything that soothes and restores.

Healing is learning to know

where to find The Mother

in her myriad forms

whenever you need her.

WHY GOD IS WOMAN

Who is it
that would have created
those curvaceous hills,
those sumptuous valleys?

Who would take the care
to create the delicate origami
of wildflower?

Whose attention to detail
would allow light access
to crawl through
even the deepest tunnels
of the Mariana Trench?

Who would have cared
to fill the chests of birds
with happy music?

Who would have weaved the tapestry

of this Universe

on that orbital loom

or been wild enough

to have slipped those dervish planets

all that celestial wine

to keep them whirling in eternal devotion

around her light?

Who would have made circles and cycles

and softness and yielding

the rule?

Who would have paused to make

the exquisite flowering

of every living thing

susceptible to light?

Who would have been luscious enough

to churn the moon?

Go on making your cars and devices, men.

I'll be praying to Goddess

as she spins me a blanket of stars.

TRY HUMAN

Forget perfection.
Go for messy, learning
tender, whole.

Forget brand new.
Embrace cracked,
broken open, worn,
rich with story.

Forget polished.
Choose rusted,
textured, nuanced, real.

Please cease
this intimidating flawlessness
and become generous
in sharing your sacred wound.
Forget Divine—
try human.

ABSORBED BY THE ROSE

What is it

that's still convincing you

of lifelessness?

Go! Be absorbed by the rose!

After an experience like that,

you'll kick and scream

and put up such a fit

before any illusion

that tries to call you back.

WHAT IF?

What would the world be like
if instead of tabloids
in waiting rooms
we had watercolors,

if doctors' offices
served strawberry juice
for free, with lime,

if elevator music
were out of the box

and lifted you up
like yodeling marimba
like Cat Stevens reggae
like a sound without walls?

What if beige meant,
"please put graffiti on me?"

and what if graffiti meant art

and God meant color

and church meant an open canvas

and Sundays, free to explore it?

What if each day of the week

were named after one of the ways

we feel under light?

What if evolution displayed

its culminating senior thesis project

in your fingertips

and God's best truth

manifested in the perfect geometry

of your eyes?

What if your eyes were my own

and when I looked in them

I'd see the hope

that's been waiting for us

to hold it

together?

CONTEMPLATING THE FLAMBOYANCE
OF A PINEAPPLE

We live in a Seussical world

where birds sing and fly

and weird roosters

welcome the dawn

and seeds

tinier than fingernails

become trees,

where people like Dr. Seuss exist

and we respond to his work

because it reminds us

of the fantastical nature

of reality

where people not only have minds

but use these things called minds

to become masters of art

to make pistachio flavored ice cream

to create airplanes

to practice understanding.

We live in a world where

clouds drink up rivers and oceans

and drop them back on our heads

and where oceans match our tears

and rain looks like tears

and sunlight and moonlight match

different moods of our hearts

and there are stars

that can't stop pinning themselves

like items of flare to the black work coat

of our universe

and where there's a Creative Force

that is cool enough

to have created giraffes

or to have created an evolution

brilliant enough to create giraffes

and wonderful enough

to have planted compassion

in the human heart

and other astounding forces

within this small, rhythmic organ

that can grow to be even more

mighty and grand

and giving

than those huge trees

grown from things

smaller than your fingernails.

G-AWE-D

I don't like the word God.

G-O-D,

God.

Two hard consonants

shut

like solid doors

around the 'O'

the Oh!

the Awe

the softly infinite.

But creak open the hard walls

around this name

as far as your hinges have learned

to give

and throw the 'G"

and the 'D'

like twigs

into whatever you want to call the enormity

of that blaze

that feeds the 'O'

the Awe

the Circle

fed brighter by all things

that once seemed to stand

in light's way.

WE NEED TO MEET AGAIN

If it's been a week

a day, even a moment

since we met

we need to meet again—

aren't you a brand new creation too?

Can this be our only binding contract:

to meet anew in the

arising wave

of each moment,

that meadow of perfect freshness?

With each glance

let us

renew our vows

again and again

at the holy altar

of complete undoing

Let us not be so stiff and un-creative

as to hold each other

to the molds of yesterday .

These souls are constantly

entering and emerging through

new chrysalises.

This ancient pair of wings

is again ready

to take

its first flight.

GOD IS GREEDY

He stuffed the robin's belly

full with song

like a spoiled boy's cheeks

with chocolate

and the sun like an overfull stocking

with light,

enough to spill over

far enough to reach you.

Don't you see

God's grabby ways?

His sunrises are a tantrum

of color,

his mountains a stubborn pout

all for your attention!

He reaches for you

through the flowers, the trees.

Go ahead and be permissive,

let him get his way.

God is greedy for your heart.

MANIACS FOR LOVE

When you feel insane

with love for another

try and point it at God—

he likes that crazy stuff

and he's the wildest of them all:

full on, too much,

completely over the top!

He's such a romancer he made springs for you,

each flower a dedication.

He's rather obsessed, really.

He made birds just to sing you

every species of love song.

He composes new galaxies

at the hope you might be even vaguely interested

and pay him a glance.

Each season is more alluring than the next—
"PLEASE NOTICE ME!" he keeps shouting
through his poetic verses
sewn into all creation.

Your heart is actually an endless book
of love poems from him
if only you'll open it.

What is meant by us being created in God's image
is that we're both
total maniacs for love.

RETURN

Another round

through the dark, narrow tunnels of healing.

I swear I've been here before

and I swore I'd never return,

but this time it's to heal the myth

that there's failure in returning.

"Relapse" into old ways

is an opportunity

for greater kindness

to newly revealed tender places.

"Regression" is a deeper look

into your soul's needs.

Darling, your life

is blossom after blossom

on the thousand petaled lotus,

lesson after lesson

in how to bow more deeply.

THE FULL MOON

"I'm quirkier than you think,"
said the moon.

"Keeping you at a distance
as I do,
lets you have all sorts
of partial, crescent ideas
about me:

that I'm beautiful,
romantic, mysterious,
brimming with elegance,
almost holy.

I've liked that image
but really, what has it done?

Up closer, you'll see
my face looks like

a mouthful of crooked teeth.
I am pocked, imperfect everywhere,
a bit grayish and drab in places,
not even round, really.

Enough infatuation.
Let's come out of denial
together.

My light doesn't even come from me,
but from a bigger, more luminous source.
Stop writing poems about me
and being such an admirer.

Come closer and let's just be
together
as we stop controlling
and just let the waves
breathe in and out.
That's the only thing
that truly makes me
full."

TELL IT LIKE IT IS

I used to think

some poets just marched

into the woods

and listed things they saw

and called that a poem.

That annoyed me.

I thought it cheap and uninspired.

But that was when I sat in the bleachers

reading other people's poetry

and scowling at it.

At least they marched

into the woods at all!

And truly

to shine your eyes,

see the beauty of things and say so

is a simple, astonishing feat.

A poem is the realization

that poetry is laid about everywhere,

that it makes itself apparent and easy,

that multiple stanzas are written

in every moment of each petal,

that buckets of inspiration

drip from the dew drop,

that muses alight everywhere

like a migration of butterflies

and reams of the most heart opening poetry

glisten in each direction

light turns her head.

So really, what else is there to do

but go outside and simply

tell it like it is.

BOTTOMLESS DRINK

What is this custom made wine

you give me

that when I drink

it turns everything

including, and perhaps especially,

all of my old foibles

and shortcomings

into pure light?

Friend, come again

and as often as you like

and let us enjoy

this bottomless drink

of each other.

POURING MOONLIGHT

You don't need to bring flowers,

my dear,

now that spring is cascading

out of my heart.

There's no need for chocolates

when you've given a taste

of innermost nectar

to the lips of my soul.

I don't need you to write me love poems,

you've led me inside of one.

Who needs romantic gestures

now that both my eyes

are pouring moonlight?

THE FLOWER

The flower

never had a to-do list,

not one day of her life.

She just pointed her whole self

toward light.

The rest

took care of itself.

HOLY TAVERN

I love how little it works

when either of us tries to be sober

with the other.

Even when we put on

our best attempt

at level-headedness

we're quickly convinced

by the Wild Drunkard

living within the other.

I love how quickly

the intoxication deepens,

each word another hearty swig.

I love my continually growing

burning thirst

for you.

And mostly I love how even

a relatively brief encounter

turns this whole otherwise

un-enchanting world

into a holy tavern.

POETRY NUN

Most days

I'd like to be a poetry nun.

Marry beauty,

devote myself to the fragrant whispers

of changing seasons,

write songs of the blazing life

within each blade of grass

sing them to the ordinary

to make it bloom,

be the scribe

to the ancient language

of the soul,

live in a mountain hermitage

with some poetry nun sisters,

pick wildflowers,

make them into crowns,

and bring gifts like this

down to people

whose hearts are hungry,

train my mind

to press clouds

into origami cranes,

fly them like healing prayers

around the world.

ASK PROPERLY

God pulled away from my heart

like taking the sunshine from the flower

to teach me an important lesson

about desire.

Of course, I utterly wilted

but thought I had to appear undemanding and accommodating,

needless.

I said something flat like, "Oh, OK, go on your way then.

I'll be just fine."

On the inside I was both burning and withering

like singed straw.

I know better now.

Next time, God,

I'll grab you by the collar and say,

"Don't you dare go! Send me a million roses

cover me with your light, drown me in your beauty again

and again

I want you! I want you! I want you!

The only thing greater than you is my desire for you. Give me

your entire heart!"

God wants us to claim our desire and learn

how to ask properly

for what we want.

WHAT DO ALL OF THESE THINGS HAVE IN COMMON?

I have believed God

to be stingy,

the moon to be prude

and unromantic, withholding,

the sun to be a greedy

hoarder of light.

What do all of these things

have in common?

My hard pit of a heart

being unwilling to receive

the astonishment

of all this great love!!

PRAYER FLAGS

The work is finally moving
out of your parents' house
to God's house.

Pack up all the baggage,
the loads of dirty laundry
you collected there

and have dragged around
your entire life
gripping tightly to your past
like a doctrine
and finally take it all over
to unload at God's place.

The beloved will unpack it all with you,
shake it out,
and you'll both have a good laugh,
"Where did you get this strange number?!"

Then God will clean them off

and hang them to dry

on a line in the sun—

making them all prayer flags.

A GREAT BURLESQUE SHOW

This life is a great burlesque show

featuring the great, wild

and alluring performance

of God—

the hidden and exposed!

"Show me more!"

our longing cries

like an audience of drooling men.

"We can't take it anymore—

take it all off!

Let us fully

inside

of your mystery!

Please get naked

and hand yourself to me—

I must touch that abundant softness!"

Oh, please find my eyes in this crowd.

This distance has become unbearable!

Invite me onto your stage

and let us dance!

HOLY HIPS

My poetry became more powerful

when I stopped being afraid of my hips,

when I found the courage and surrender

to enter that sacred basin,

that gourd of creation

where it's all going down.

I found rage there, first,

then terror,

grief

and despair,

then the most aching, sacred longing—

that exquisite string

almost played

that would complete the melody of my own soul.

Power was there too,

and pleasure.

Really, everything relegated to the shadows

was found in the sway

of my sexy, playful, audacious, beautiful hips:

deep happiness and hunger, those juicy gifts

greatly deprived

of returning to our wholeness,

the storehouse of my great grandmothers' shames,

every holy but denigrated taboo,

all the tender, human

stuffed down secrets

beseeching from the dark,

"BRING ME HOME AT LAST

AND LET ME BE SEEN AND HONORED!"

And at last the flame

of my own wild song

God sung into me when I was first

conjured up.

The recipe is simple:

shake these holy hips and make this world

a sacred conflagration.

THE SACRED, WILD BARREL

Oh world,

I've been trying to convince you

of my sanity for far too long!

Trying to hold it together,

play the part.

I'm ready for the sacred undoing!

I'm ready to give up the game

I'm delighted to say

I've lost.

Here is my raw, naked heart

my soul is ready to strip down

and streak through social conventions!

I am tired of pretending with you

that I'm OK with anything short of the sweetest,

most tender intimacy.

I'm un-signing my name

from these social contracts

enabling extreme blandness and terrible distance

from our hearts!

Come close and I will kiss your face,

come closer and I will offer you

every jewel in my soul,

come closer still and I'll delightedly

give you my very life

and then rummage through my closets

to see what else I have in there for you!

Friend, it doesn't take much

to destroy social norms.

All it really takes is to crack open

the sacred, wild barrel

of love in your chest

and offer it to whomsoever

might pass by.

NAME DROP GODS

For years I thought I had to name drop Hindu Gods

for my poetry to be valid,

but I hadn't really met any yet.

I thought I needed to read all the sacred scriptures,

but they were all so dense and cumbersome!

Perhaps if I listed a couple yoga pose names—yes,

any kind of Sanskrit must be the key

to making my words spiritual and enlightened!

Be a bit more esoteric, Chelan,

a bit harder to unravel. Make your poetry

a necklace of tangled prayer beads—

your readers will want to extract God more

from your poetry for not being able to access it!

Well, thank God all that changed.

And thank God it turns out

all scripture, every spiritual encounter, every holy ordinance

is repeating the same, universal, simplicity over and over

and over:

It's either saying,

"Open your heart"

or nothing at all.

REDEFINE EVERYTHING

Un-cinch the strings

around the word 'faith'.

Take the corset

off of God.

What happens to it

when you set it free

and let it prance about?

Loosen up reverence

what happens there?

Experiment

with tickling the chin

of your beliefs

'til they crack open slightly

with joy.

What if religion

were the untying

of old knots?

Why not redefine everything

starting with the concepts

we seem to care about the most?

Let's keep reworking these definitions

until they feel more like they're meant to—

a song of untethered love.

WILD ORDER

Your controlling ways
are actually quite crude
compared to the way grace works.

Look how the earth
has let herself go
and somehow
the flower is drawn.

It turns out your willpower,
all that efforting,
is astoundingly weak
compared to the easeful way
beauty shares herself
through the form of hummingbird.

Your perfectionism
is quite a rough attempt

compared to the wild order

of the leaf.

None of the small tendencies within you

can begin to compete

with the mastery that comes

through everything surrendered.

There's a bigger you

waiting in there!

Now, slow down

pull your life over

and put all your intention

on giving yourself over

to that.

READ THE FINE PRINT

Some days I awaken so certain

of the world's goodness.

This poem is a reminder for those other days

when I need to convince my stubborn mind

that all is still well.

Let me present the evidence:

have you noticed

all the fastidious care

that went into pinning up

so many stars

to decorate the night sky?

What did that?

And the way all of nature

has a tidiness to it

even gnarled trees, even dirt?

Or sit a moment and puzzle

over the masterful origami

of each flower and think,

"what cosmic interior decorator

chose that gold

for those rolling hills?"

And before that,

who thought up tenderness?

Who is it that came up

with all these colors

and what genius said, "Autumn"?

My only simple conclusion

as I sit amazed at the pileup of gifts

is that we're part of a great

contract of goodness

and there's love

written into every atom

if you get close enough

to read the fine print.

LOVE AWAITS YOU THERE

It's easier to notice pain than love.

Love is the silence

in the robin's throat

that inspires it to sing.

Love is the silent mantra of the Universe

that keeps things spinning.

Pain is the tree that crashes in the forest,

love is what grows from the fallen.

Love is the silence cupped

in the perfect folds of an autumn leaf,

the beauty that dances through everything

when your worried mind has finally stilled.

We forget to notice love

because of its perfect loyalty:

morning dew diamonding the grass,

the extra sparkle in snow—

for what other reason need it be there?—

the unconditional warmth arising daily to fill your sky,

the ongoingness of flowers.

Pause, dear one,

love awaits you there.

REBELLIOUS SECRETARIES

What God wants

is for us all to become

rebellious secretaries

unlabeling every bit

of our hearts

and this indescribably

beautiful world.

GOD OF JOY

I've come to you,

oh God of Joy.

I've made you my destination

and you are here and now

and that is where I'll stop

my heavy travels

and hand myself over.

I'm done winding

the long, scraggly miles

after a God of crusts

and poor returns.

You, God, of true wine

and jubilance,

I've chosen your feast.

I will no longer turn myself

away from the table

and blame my stingy

version of you

for my hunger.

I'm sitting,

I'm staying

and I'm ready for all the courses.

Now, please, Lord,

pass those buttery potatoes.

WHIRLING FESTIVAL

You won't ever get it all done.

Leaves will continue

to fall all over the forest floor

just when summer thinks

she's gotten everything cleaned up.

Please don't try so hard

to keep it all in!

Blossoms will one day

shoot their wild-headed ideas out

of what used to be their tight,

orderly, self-contained buds

and every year the trees

become hippies

sharing the free love

of their juicy, fruity creations

with anyone who desires!

Darling, you are part of this wild design

and it's okay to let go a bit.

Try putting a jig

in the step of your soul

and join this whirling festival

of all that is

in the dance of the undone

and ever becoming.

ECSTATIC SPARK

Darling, I've seen

the hyper-vigilance of tight reins

you use to hold back your frothing soul

from racing toward what it loves.

And while I understand your hesitation,

I pray

that this Wild-Haired Universe will grab you close,

hold you to her chest and whisper,

"This life is a brief,

ecstatic spark.

Darling, fling yourself into the stars."

A LITTLE MORE OFTEN

When I'm feeling uninspired

I call on the great, mystical

and irreverent poet, Hafiz

and ask him to remind me

to stop being so serious

and pinch God's butt

a little more often.

YOUR OWN DAMN JOY

The price of admission

into heaven

is your own damn joy.

Please stop denying yourself this

and please stop telling yourself

you'll only (maybe) get there when you die—

go there now!

What kind of damn fool

puts off heaven?

Child, it lives in the center of your heart

that endless meadow of happiness and praise.

This world needs you

to go there now

to do your part in turning it

into a paradise.

START ANYWHERE

The paralysis of choice

is like freezing up

at the blueberry bush.

Fool!

Wrong doesn't exist here!

Just the abundant sampling

of experience.

This world is hanging

with delicious options—

start anywhere.

POETRY CLASS

Drop yourself off in the woods.

Leave yourself there.

Erase your heart

of its to-do lists.

Become part of the forest

at whatever level:

tree, snag, log, sapling.

Know that you too have bark

that protects you from

the beetles of life

and that's okay

but feel under it

growth lives there,

life lives there.

Go on and speak

what your heart sees.

Say, "Here! Here is my poem!"

Watch it grow, leaf, blossom

wilt, decompose, grow again

and flower through you

and say, "Here, here!

I am the poem."

IRRESISTIBLE MUSIC!

Put golden shoes

on your prayers.

Let your feet start

tapping with hidden delight.

Cut the middle out of your holy robes,

let God catch a glimpse of midriff—

that'll get him excited

to see you finally loosening up!

Invite the sway

back into your hips.

Your devotion is for naught

if your soul doesn't move

with this irresistible music!

AN ENTHUSIASTIC "YES!"

God reaches out to you
with alluring offers, regularly,

through the tender touch
of a newly opened flower
handing all of its sweetness
to your dear eyes,

through the playful and beckoning invitation
of the meadow, calling,
"enter all of me at once!"

to the bubbling spring ever asking
your soul to undress,
take a dip,

through every fire saying,
"I long to touch your whole body
with my warmth!"

But God is respectful
and cares about your consent
and you have yet to give
an enthusiastic "Yes!"

You've been wandering around
with a chastity belt on your mind,
keeping respectable and loveless.

Darling, drop the front!
Every full, juicy atom
of this fertile world
knows your secret desire
to finally say that wide open "Yes!"
to the come-ons
of the Great Beloved!

RAIN DANCE

Search

for the best possible

human love

and when even that proves

unsatisfactory

your heart will become a desert

so parched for God

and the dry earth of your being

so desperate to be quenched

that it'll turn your every movement

into a prayer—

the rest of your life

will become a rain dance

beseeching Divine showers.

NOTHING IS TRULY AN ORIGINAL

Nothing is truly an original.

The delicate curl and color

of leaves write most of the poetry,

flowers write the rest.

Can I take credit

for celestial rascals

pouring buckets of light

down for me to capture

and bring to a space where

love can echo?

I often plagiarize breath,

who does most of the work,

and the collage of all those beautiful

eyes I've looked into,

her cheeks,

the way that tree arcs her longing,

the song of the world saying its last words

to summer's soft face.

So who am I to credit these poems to?

Light doesn't need to sign its name.

DON'T COMPARTMENTALIZE GOD

Don't compartmentalize God.

Do you think this permeating essence

only stays in the clouds

or is snooty enough to only

tolerate light?

God does not live outside

the mundane.

She encircles and infuses

every ordinary thing.

She smears her grace liberally

over every excess.

God is bidirectional

not only up

but down and in

to the nectarous center

of every wound.

God does not disallow herself entrance

into any darkness.

She dives headlong into the profane.

Do you imagine she abides

any kind of caution tape?

She kisses the heart

of every misdeed,

she drinks deep of your dark song,

she undoes every binary

and the very notion of wrongness,

she discovers tenderness

in the nucleus of every sin.

If light has never hidden its face

from any darkness

then what of its creator?

A TASTE

How dare you break the social code?!
All of our addictions are held in this box!

How dare you move outside the bounds?!
The grace of your movement might invoke my own

inner goddess

to dance fissures in my facade!

How dare you speak power
to my fastidiously constructed fragility?!

How dare you let your beauty flow into mine
reminding me how far I've been from joy?!

How dare you push up through the pavement, flower,

exposing all its cracks?!

How dare you let go of pretense enough
to feel the rush of soul

that geyser of sweet sorrow and light

and how dare you allow me to feel

how thirsty I've been for a taste?

TROVE

What I want to do

with my life

is open the trove

of my heart

again and again

and again.

There is nothing

of greater value to be found

than delighting

in these treasures.

DEAD ARTIST

With love

the moon and the stars

were warm faces I could touch.

Now they're a hands-off exhibit

in the cold, sterile museum of the sky

created by God,

that dead artist.

NO MORE ECSTATIC LOVE POEMS

No more ecstatic love poems.

No more describing the stars

as a string of bejeweled prayer beads

for God's mantra.

Tonight, I want the black stone

of my pain

to go unpolished.

No more convincing you to adore

my shards of light

the ones too sharp to get close to.

Tonight my poems are not divine love songs—

my heart is a wolf

yowling at the cold

unreciprocating moon.

NECTAROUS ONES

Oh nectarous ones!

You with an abundance of God

spilling out of your hearts!

Ones who have allowed the sacred seed

to enter the dark soil

of your most fertile shadows,

who have let the Divine Kiss be planted

within you and for the rest of you to continually

break open

in the process of this flowering—

thank you!

It hasn't been holy doctrines that have done it—

you are my best access points.

You have shown me this way.

GOD BROKE IN LAST NIGHT

God broke in last night

and what once used to be

my put together soul

has now become a holy mess!

Thank God, the Great Scrambler,

the Ransacker of Every Bit of the Small-Self,

the Demolition Artist of the Best Laid Plans ,

the Intolerant of Too Tidy,

the Frustrated with Facade,

The Broken Pot!

I'll pray to you in a new way now—

it no longer seems perfection

is what we're getting at.

JUST AS HOLY

The stars are pieces
of God's broken heart.

Because she didn't scurry
to clean them up quickly—
make the universe all tidy for its company—
and just let herself be
a shimmering, perfect mess

the poetry of worlds
was allowed to bloom.
Do the same with your heart,
dear one.

Your process is just
as holy.

DON'T GET IT BACKWARD

Don't get it backward

God, if anything, is frustrated with your perfection.

It's through the cracked open mess

of your soul

that she can finally express

her poetry,

her wild song,

her own aching heart.

THE WOUND

The only advice I have for you

is to not fix the wound.

The sirens of your pain will call you in

again and again,

please stop resisting them.

When you allow this deep dive

to retrieve your laughter, your tears,

your prayers, your song, your poetry

you are communicating the language of the soul

to this forgetful world.

SELF-CARE

Perhaps we need to give dimension
to the meaning of self-care.

Self-care can mean finally sinking
into the dark pools of your shadows
you've long avoided.

Self-care can mean encountering
the self-spun and inherited veils
we've cloaked over our luminous spirit
and inquiring,
"Am I more than that?"

Self-care can mean at last entering
the forest of your terrors
to realize the fears you'd othered
are all howling like night animals
within you
and realizing the outside was always within

brings new wisdom.

Self-care can mean finally
looking yourself in the eyes,
into the black holes of your pupils
and their wild desire to annihilate
every untruth you've held dear.

And within all this, self-care can still mean
we get to eat a little extra chocolate.

POLLINATED WITH LONGING

You've pollinated me with longing
and now there is no rest!

You've exposed my distance
to the inmost heart of God
and now I'm desperate to find refuge there!

If my heart needs to lighten its load, no worries
my last holdout, sanity, has long since been cast out.

Is this what you want?
to agitate our souls to such a degree
that we cannot, even for one moment,

stop singing to you?

"WILL YOU LOVE ME BACK?"

God, I want you with a fervent longing!

Come into my bones!

My tinder box is set,

all it'll take is one spark.

I can no longer handle this absence!

The house of my soul

has been vacant for too long.

Open all of my doors

and enter every room of me

at once.

The mundanities of living without you

have been exposed

and now there's no true returning

to this distant rock of a world.

Put the sun in my heart.

Unlock all verdure and holiness.

I want to be put in my rightful orbit,

dedicate an eternity

to dancing wild circles around you.

I'm ready to do all it takes to open

I just need you to answer my one final question:

"Will you love me back?"

YOU MUST LOVE

You must love freedom enough
to embrace confinement.

You must adore the ecstatic enough
to integrate the mundane.

You must be so inebriated with joy
that you welcome all sorrow.

you must be so desirous of wholeness
that all your fragments reunite.

You must yearn for home with such a yearning
that your exiled pieces may return.

You must love transcendence enough to allow the truth
that transcendence is inclusive of all prior limitations.
Your open heart remembers its brokenness,
the blossom does not shun the bud.

ADJUST, DEAR ONE!

We are always in deep
and focused meditation
and prayer practice.

It's simply that our fixated attention
happens to often be on things
that don't serve us!

And our prayer, the stories that run
through our mind and conduct
the energy of our heart,
are often requesting undesirables!

Adjust, dear one!
All goodness lies awaiting
in the untapped treasure chest
of you

and you're already doing everything

you're meant to with expertise!

It's simply time to discover

you have choice

about where to point

your tremendous power!

PLEASE

Our deeply held wounds

are buds

simply requesting,

"Please, bring me to light."

RE-WILD GOD

Oh Wild God,

Caster Out of Doctrines,

Scatterer of Seeds,

Heart Thirsty Drunkard,

Forgiver of Worsts,

Opener of Blossoms ,

Softest Home to Every Frailty,

Uprooter of Untruths,

Bather in Darkness,

Recoverer of the Most Hidden Lights—

You

are the only one I have ever sought.

UNTAME YOUR GOD

Untame your God.
Let her run through the wilderness
of your soul again.

Allow her to take off all her clothes—
enough with modesty—

she wants to pound her chest
and drink moonlight through you.

Let her re-invoke the stars
back into each cell
and give them all wine.

Allow her to unapologetically
sever every cord of control
and let you feel how tender freedom is,
how loving you can be without obeying
anything but the pulsing truth

that's eternally yearned

to sing out from your heart

inviting magic home.

SUNKEN SHIPS

The ocean of your soul

longs for you to enter its depths

and bring up the sunken ships

of your old emotions,

recycle them into new

seaworthy vessels,

reclaim their lost treasures

and show you there is nothing to uncover

in even your deepest trenches

that can keep you from wholeness.

PLEASE DON'T TRY

Please don't try

to hurry through this meadow

toward ambition,

ease, pleasure,

lunch.

Please don't try

to hurry through the intimate,

fiery lick of pain

or the cauldron of heartbreak

slowly brewing you into new magic.

Please don't wait

for the grandeur,

the fabulous vistas,

when all the richness of the now

is at your fingertips

ready to be gathered into your heart.

Don't move toward love,

move with it

it's in you

you are it!

What are you waiting for,

blind desirer!

The object of your goal has always been

exactly where you stand.

GOD WILL BREAK YOUR HEART

God will break your heart

when she's hungry

for a new, open space

to sing through.

SACRED BRUTE

Love is a sacred brute
she'll break into any heart
more or less uninvited
and bring up every well hidden wound.

She'll take your pacifiers one by one,
if she's kind
or the whole bundle all at once,
if not.

She is imprudent, manner-less
a deity of wreckage
to every comfortable structure.

She does not care about maintaining you
anything like you were.

She is a vandal to every tidiness.
She opens

your well-stored inner boxes

and giddily loosens your collection

of rage and griplessness.

Her only intention?

To fully take off your mask

so God's face can finally

shine through you.

CLAUSTROPHOBIC

God's been getting a bit claustrophobic

in the tight confines of your heart—

look out!

She might bring grief, loss

any form of heartbreak

to crack things open

get a bit more spaciousness

to accommodate her wider dance.

ON I GO!

"I came to this earth so that I could find my way back to my

beloved." —Rumi

Indeed,

and not only do we get

to find our way back

but to do it so richly!

There's the aroma

of coffee, for one,

and also pine trees

after the rain

and honeysuckle!

And beetles,

with their hard, shiny shields

and rich soil

where tiny seeds

burst out

into sprawling bouquets

and stars

and Mothers

and raindrops

and joy.

This "Way" Rumi has mentioned,

I like it very much—

on I go!

SLAY YOUR SACRED COWS

God smiles, almost bemoaningly,

at your stack of prayers,

your hoard of good deeds,

your performed purity,

gives a big, celestial "sigh".

If he could sit you down and give you a good talk,

that is, if he didn't have better things to do

like whirl and celebrate his own great mystery

and rapturously

create universes and such

he would say,

"Darlin', you have to slay your sacred cows first.

You must stop kissing ass, even mine,

especially mine.

You must plunge into this soul I gave you—

it is deep, terrifying and wondrous.

You must stop hesitating.
You must nourish yourself
and forget everything
you've been taught in church
and everywhere else.

Your soul is the sacred tome,
these books are simply arrows
back into you.

You must actively strip your soul,
skinny dip in me.
Feel the grace, experience the touch
of mystical astonishment
for your own self—
I didn't make you a sheep!

I made you a sorcerer of wisdom,
a slayer of untruths,
a vessel of stars,
a fortress of inner knowing,
a cathedral of beauty.

To get to me you must slay your sacred cows.

To get to me you must first be willing

to slay everything

you've thought me to be."

FAVORITE FLUTES

That spirit that sang through Rumi

and Hafiz

was not confined to them.

That playful and poignant spirit

that tickles and caresses hearts open

with the same hand of invisible grace

and gentleness that opens the rose—

it sings through many these days.

In fact, I think I know a few

of its favorite flutes.

JUST SMITTEN

My name is Chelan

and I am wildly

in love

with The Divine.

Just smitten.

There. I said it!

Plenty of us are in denial

of this basic joy

of our existence.

Come out of your spiritual closet,

dear one.

I'm afraid the effort it takes

to repress a jewel

like this

might make you sick.

IT'S A GOOD DAY

This life

is but one mighty day.

We've been spinning around the sun

dipping into darkness and rising

around and around.

In this one big, beautiful day

of gathering love

in all its shades

we get to be both children

and elders,

we get to be playful,

we get to be part of beauty,

we become kneaded with meaning,

we get to serve something higher.

This one day is spinning us all

into lovers of this great light

that the immense brilliance of the sun

is only hinting at—

it's a good day.

WHAT THE HELL IS GOING ON!?

Don't worry

you're new at this

we all are!

Being human,

having a body,

having a mind,

learning about how

to work with a soul?!

What is happiness?

What is love?

It's ok to ask any question.

We are all such beginners

in this life thing,

little zygotes

developing inside

of a vast mystery.

Be kind to the parts of you

that have never known

what the hell is going on!

8 DAYS A WEEK

What God wants for us

is to find something that we love

8 days a week

and to sing our praises

through that.

This is what the bee told me

as she spent her whole afternoon

kissing the sweet spot

of flowers.

THE INTERNAL SEASON

There is an elegance

in timing

that nothing can teach you

so well as spring.

The way she summons flowers open

with the magical finesse

of light, her touch

never skipping over the face

of even one buttercup.

It's hard to trust the sun

when you've been

gone from her so long, I know,

but spring is an internal season

and she is not an abandoner.

Be patient with your flowering, sweet pea,

the agony of waiting

is part of the blossom.

A HAT

Even after all

these run-ins with God

some days my heart is still

a hat on the pavement

begging for change

and today my soul

does not know

when it will get its next meal.

THE SECOND WAY

Sometimes my poems

are just flat

pieces of paper

with scrawls on them

and other times

they're directions

to fold that ordinary flatness

into origamied cranes

that can fly into

the heart

and dimensionalize it.

Sometimes the stars are

discarded notes

of God's bad ideas

crinkled up and thrown aside

and other times they're a universe

of dazzling suns.

It makes me wonder

about what leads me to see things

the second way.

✤

STUBBORN RESISTANCE

It's okay if you're scared

when you're opening.

The seed,

she was scared too.

Do you think the coal

wanted to become

a diamond?

Ha!

She was scared

out of her wits

of change!

It took her 10,000 years

to even be able

to pray for it.

And what about

our favorite cliché, the caterpillar?

You must have heard

his shrieks of resistance

as some bigger force

unwelcomely impelled it

to eat its own form

while disclosing nothing

of those secret wings.

The acorn

was so stodgy,

the far-right

of the plant kingdom

100% closed in by the hard walls

of its staunch beliefs.

My-oh-my did he resist

becoming the regal, generous oak.

The only thing different in us

from them

is we have an even more

stubborn resistance

but ultimately

we are impelled

by the same irresistible force

to completely self-destruct

into a New and Improved

Yet to be Discovered Marvel.

Do your best to allow this—

you too were made for wings.

UNPLEASANT CONFRONTATION

Fear is a parasite.

It's been slipping through the house

of your being like a shadow

living off of you,

that freeloader!

And you

looking the other way,

working around it,

have been its enabler.

It seems that it's time

to look things

in the eye,

stop keeping the "peace"

and get ready

for an unpleasant confrontation.

THE TOAST

I say it's time to realize

that we hold a sloshing

amount of light

in the cup of each cell

and some Divine Party Animal within

continues to raise us

like a glass of joy

in a toast of celebration

to the wonder of being—

Cheers!

"JUDGMENT DAY"

What if "Judgment Day"

consists of grouping together

all the people you acted in dumb ways around

in this absurd life

as you were waking up from those damn fool ways

we are all waking up from, by the way,

and laughing and grieving our hearts

back into tenderness

together

now that we finally

understand?

I'M YOURS

God, this is another
tattered heart prayer
and my work is to remember
that you accept
this kind of currency.

I had closed myself off to you
for so long
waiting to arrive
in fashionable robes
(impress you a bit)

and wait to get rich enough
to display handfuls of gold
to you!
Ha!

I thought you'd like it better
that way.

Can we sit on the floor

and laugh together about this

now?

Of course,

You never wanted any of that

but just for me

to grow

into the honesty of my heart

like sweetness

into a plum

and bring myself to you

tangled but entire

And say,

"God, in robes or rags,

I'm yours."

THEY ARE GROWING

Hold your mistakes

like a baby.

Look into their eyes

into the innocence, the hope

that lives deep

inside them.

Don't throw them out—

they are of you

and they are growing.

O GOD

In this unyielding world

I want to be supple enough

to hold you.

SWINGING DOORS

Turn your beliefs

into swinging doors.

Open wide!

There's light

on both sides.

WHAT IF WE TOLD THE FLOWER

What if we told the flower,

"don't bloom"

and told the birds,

"don't sing"

and told the petals,

"don't you dare show your tenderness"

and told the bee

kissing the sweetest

part of the rose's heart

"it's uncomfortable to see

love given so freely"

and told the stars

"don't shine, it'll make someone scared"

and told the quivering bunny

holding itself beneath shivering winds

"toughen up"

and told the morning sun

shining over slowly waking hills

enlivening everything,

"stop showing off"

and told the music within the wind to

"keep its voice down."

These are the messages that have been given

to our souls

and quite frankly,

these ideas

really suck.

THE HALLWAY

What if there's

no such thing

as ignorance,

but just

a long series

of doors

in the hallway

towards light?

THE WAY THE ROSE MAKES AMENDS

There are times I feel

that I need to make amends

with every person in my life.

There is no person

the blanket of my unconsciousness

has not touched

in some way.

But with perspective I see

the flower

does not need to apologize

for her tight, rigid stem,

the same one helping her

upwards toward light

or the rose, on her way to herself,

for her thorns.

When the blossom comes

all of the past is understood,

all is forgiven

in a single gush

of openness.

DON'T RUIN UGLINESS

Don't stop being vain,

start painting.

Don't lose weight,

gain movement

and eat more

strawberries.

Don't silence your ego

but start to fill

its big, gaping mouth

with deeper breath.

Don't worry about self-absorption,

say thank you to the flowers before you pick them.

It's not fun

this practice of self-hate

but if you must continue it,

before the "I" finds itself

a bigger pastime,

do it with complete confidence

after you try and tell the sun,

the bluebird,

the total perfection

of the unbelievably delicate

falling leaf

how much you hate all of them

first.

SACRED TEARS

Sacred Tears

soul diamonds

14-carat truths

God proposing marriage

to your

wholeness.

MAGIC SHOW

Cancel everything.

Go sit in your yard.

Make sunshine

a priority.

Turn your to-do list into

whatever happens next.

That's when the Universe

invites you to her magic show

of exactly what is.

THE REASON I'M HOPEFUL

The reason I'm hopeful

is because I've never seen a tree

that grows backward,

never known a flower

to scurry away

from light

and I think the human spirit

to have even more

light thirsty petals

and an even stronger

and more determined

trunk.

BASK IN THAT

You are doing enough
by growing basil in your front yard
and delighting in it.

You are doing enough
by sitting still
and saying "thanks"
to whatever's around you.

You are doing enough
with this breath
and that one too.

You are doing enough
by being the canvas
for all the intricate and unique designs
love draws within the heart.

You are doing enough

by sampling all the flavors

of light.

Go ahead and take a break.

You've been invited to an orb

of mystery and joy!

Whoever says you can't bask in that

was just trying to use you

to make him more money.

COME HOME

First I tried to cut out fat

then eliminate sugar,

then it went to my shadows.

I tried to dust them all off

clean out my cellars.

I kept trying to perfect every corner

of my being:

health, relationship, spiritual life

and it wasn't working.

Darling, stop trying so hard,

that's so often the answer.

Just give your mess

a warm place to come home to.

✤

DRINK THAT

I caught myself today
trying to be controlling
while this great, wild globe of a world,
I'm just hitching a ride on, spun madly
deepening its tracks through the unknown.

There's a part of this charade that's amusing,
watching myself try to perfect my house, my life, my husband
while the trees keep giddily throwing armfuls of leaves on the
ground
reminding me that nothing
is ever completely swept up here.

Look outside— even flowers are unruly!
Uncorking their buds as they do
to let blossom burst through like colorful champagne
and stars act like children
pouring their golden paint with abandon
all over the slick black floor of the universe.

There's an immaculate harmony of chaos and order

that when well mixed becomes beauty—

stir yourself with laughter

and drink that.

FORGIVE YOURSELF

Forgive yourself.

All of your faults

have a root in something tender.

WALK ON

Dust clings to snow,

that symbol of purity.

Shade grips to light.

Why is it, dear,

you try so hard to separate

your human struggles

from your luminous spirit?

Don't they accept one another?

How desperate the night would be

if it weren't studded with stars

and how grotesque the beaming day

if it weren't followed by the luxurious elegance

of darkness?

Imagine if you spent each walk

obsessing with stripping yourself

of your shadow—

there's more to focus on.

You were made like this,

walk on.

THE PINEAPPLE

The gnarled tree with limbs going every which way

grabbing at sunlight from all directions to nourish its crooked

body,

the rose, elegant and defensive,

hyper-vigilant in her thorns,

the pineapple, scaly, yellow and flamboyant

with that stiff, green-leafed hairdo sticking straight up,

the violet, tender and timid,

and even the cactus that won't let anyone touch it—

they all whisper the same thing:

"It's okay to be all of you,

just as you are."

MIGRATING BIRD

The oil was running low
in the lamp in my chest,

the flower of my poetry
needed water

and life had become
more a series of chores
than an unfoldment of wonders

more a list
than a song.

So of course, something in my soul
invoked you
like the warm call of the south
to the soul of a bird.

And though, like the south,

I can't keep you, my beautiful,

migrating bird

the echos of your warble

are what will keep something

in the center of my sun shining

and part of me will always

be calling for you.

BETTER THINGS TO DO

God isn't some hovering weirdo.

The Divine Entity must have better things to do

than frown upon every ignorant deed.

Surely, this God

is more interested in the magical,

generative works

of luring things toward light.

Break your mental images of God,

those fearful little knick-knacks

that line the shelves of your mind

and go on and let this God-Thing

become the Great Mystery within

the unfolding sunrise

in your heart.

ANCESTRAL TREASURE

Your ancestors have passed down
their wounds like a growing collection of gems
for your inheritance—
don't resent this.

They weren't ready to be mined and collected,
they weren't ready to be valued.

You have the technology now.
You know how to dig deep.
You know now how not
to fear your worth.

You know that within every bright, shining wound
is a nugget of compassion,
a jewel of wisdom.
They have saved up for you.
Now feel deeply blessed
to be driven, finally, into these inner tunnels

of self and history.

Cashing in on this trove
in the sacred chest of your heart
will alchemize all old, shameful stories
into diamonds of laughter and tears.

Cashing in this trove
will transform the heavy bag of sorrows your ancestor carried
into tokens of priceless light.

MORNING GLORY

Sometimes it's better

to pray with your eyes open

to see the hummingbirds

buzzing around like golden snitches

in search of morning nectar

or watch dawn

begin to drape

her diaphanous, light woven shawl

over the landscape

of your heart and mind.

Sometimes it's better

to pray with your mouth closed

to give your soul a platform

to listen to the seas of beauty

pulsing within silence.

Perhaps what I'm saying is that

prayer is an invitation

to let go of format,

and enter the holy bones

of your body's sweet temple

and that whatever tongue, whatever movement

whatever way your longing pulls you to connect

with the sacred, "Wow"

that is always sitting deep within your chest—

that is holy,

that is prayer.

LET US DANCE

Your smarts, your talents, your good looks—

take off these impediments

and let us dance!

ABOUT THE AUTHOR

Chelan has always had a close connection with the spiritual world, a loving, ecstatic and expressive spirit, and an intimacy in her soul that she longs to share with others and the whole world. Poetry is one of her favorite, most satisfying ways to accomplish this.

Her process with poetry is very special to her. All of these poems have come through essentially intact and entire in less than two minutes with little to no content editing. Chelan believes they are luminous morsels of remembrance from the spiritual world to help her on her way and to share with others. One of the gifts of this poetry is the deconstructing of old ideas of God that haven't served us in hopes of a warmer, closer, more authentic relationship with the divine and with our inmost hearts. She adores her readers. You fan her flame. Stay tuned and get excited for upcoming book, *Let Us Dance: The Stumble and Whirl with the Beloved.*

Made in the USA
Monee, IL
27 December 2020

55703559R00121